SURPRISING SWIMMERS

by Anthony D. Fredericks

NorthWord

NORTHWORD PRESS, INC.
Minocqua, Wisconsin

DEDICATION

For my daughter Rebecca—

with love and pride

ACKNOWLEDGMENTS

A special note of thanks to

Paula Gilbert—the world's

greatest children's librarian—

for her efforts in making

this dream possible.

Photography © 1996 by: Frans Lanting/Minden Pictures, 3, 11. Pacific Stock: Steve Rosenberg, 4; Carl Roesseler, 5; David Fleetham, 7, 8, 27; Jim Watt, 23. Runk/Schoenberger/Grant Heilman Photography, 13. Flip Nicklin/Minden Pictures, 15. Norbert Wu, 17, 29. Tom Stack & Associates: David Dennis, Cover; Jeff Foott, 19; David Fleetham, 24. G. Prance/Visuals Unlimited, 21. Fritz Polking/Dembinsky Photo Associates, 31.

NorthWord Press, Inc.
P.O. Box 1360
Minocqua, WI 54548

Illustrations by Kay Povelite
Book design by Lisa Moore

Library of Congress Cataloging-in-Publication Data

Fredericks, Anthony D.
      Surprising swimmers / by Anthony D. Fredericks.
          p.   cm. — (World of discovery)
      Summary: Describes why and how such creatures as squids, scallops, devil fish, and sea otters swim—for protection, for pleasure, and to get around.
        ISBN 1-55971-543-X (hardcover)
         1. Animal swimming—Juvenile literature.   [1. Animal swimming.]
      I. Title.   II. Series.
      QP310.S95F74 1996
      591.1'852—dc20
                                         95-35667

Printed in Hong Kong

SURPRISING SWIMMERS

CONTENTS

Marine Iguana

About Swimmers

Sea Otter

Have you ever been to a pool, a lake, or the ocean to go swimming? Swimming is one of the most enjoyable activities we do. We swim to cool off during a hot day, we swim for exercise and relaxation, and we swim to get from one place to another (to cross a lake, for example). Everybody, young or old, enjoys swimming.

Sea Snake

Many animals swim, too. Fish swim, birds swim, reptiles and amphibians swim, and mammals and insects swim. Animals swim for different reasons. For example, for dolphins, swimming is their primary form of locomotion, or travel. Ducks swim to locate food. For frogs, swimming is a way to escape from enemies. Salmon have to swim in order to mate. And, like you, some animals (including bears) swim for relaxation.

As you know, there are many ways to swim. Animals may swim on top of the water or under the water. Some animals swim 24 hours a day. Some swim in unusual ways. Still others are clumsy in their attempts to swim—have you ever seen a dog paddle? Some animals are natural swimmers; for others, it does not come so easily. There are, however, several animals whose swimming ability is nothing less than amazing!

In this book, you will have a chance to meet some of the most unusual swimmers in the animal kingdom. You will read about a lizard, a bird, and a spider, each of which can swim underwater. You will also learn about a snail and a snake, both of which can swim on top of the water. And you'll read about an insect that can swim backward! As you read, think about why a particular animal swims as it does and how its swimming ability helps it survive in the wild. You're sure to discover some fascinating facts about these 12 surprising swimmers of the animal world.

Squids live in a variety of habitats throughout the world's oceans—from the warm waters of the tropics to the colder regions of the Atlantic and Pacific. In some countries, squid is prized as a food delicacy. As a result, squids have become endangered animals in some parts of the world.

Rocket Racers

The fastest a human being can swim is about 5 mph. If you were in a car going 5 mph you would think you were traveling quite slowly. But there's an animal that can swim six times faster than a human—up to 30 mph—and it's able to do it backward! This jet-propelled creature is the squid.

Size for size, a squid can outswim almost every other marine animal. It's able to do this because its rocket-shaped body is well suited for racing at high speeds. The squid's streamlined body also has powerful muscles that contract to force out a jet of water just like a blast from a fire hose.

These blasts occur repeatedly, allowing the squid to zig and zag through the water looking for food.

Like its cousin the octopus, a squid has eight arms covered with powerful suckers. In addition, it also has two tentacles (arms) that are used to capture small fish, crabs, and other sea creatures. When a fish is caught, the squid kills it with a bite from its mighty beak. It then removes the head of the fish and strips the flesh from its bones.

Squids are also noted for their excellent eyesight, which is more advanced than that of any other invertebrate (it has no backbone) in the animal kingdom. Not only does their eyesight help them locate food, but it also helps squids identify approaching enemies. When an enemy is sighted, squids protect themselves by emitting an inky fluid, and then dart from their pursuer into the cloudy water. As additional protection, squids can also change their colors, especially when excited.

A rocket-powered sea creature! An animal that can change its color whenever it wants to! Excellent eyesight and strong muscles! The squid must be a very intelligent creature because, like you, it is frequently found in schools.

The famous giant squid of the Atlantic Ocean reaches a length of 50 feet and a weight of 2 tons. Its eyes are the size of basketballs!

The fire squid of the Indian Ocean has organs that flash light in different colors— blue, green, white, and red.

Slithering Sea Serpent

Sea snakes can be found from the Persian Gulf to Japan and south to Australia. They live in coral reefs, river mouths, mangrove swamps, and the open ocean. Like their land relatives, they come in a variety of colors. The most common are bright yellow with black markings.

Life in the ocean is sometimes difficult. Animals must be able to get their own food without becoming food for someone else. Many marine creatures have learned how to adapt to this frequently harsh environment by developing special skills or body parts that allow them to grow, develop, and reproduce for many generations. Certainly one of the most distinctive animals of this aquatic ecosystem is the sea snake.

Just like its cousins on land, the sea snake has developed specific features that help it survive. These creatures spend their entire lives in the ocean. As a result, their bodies are flattened side to side—a feature that allows them to travel through the water with ease. Their tails, shaped like the oars on a rowboat, also contribute to their swimming prowess.

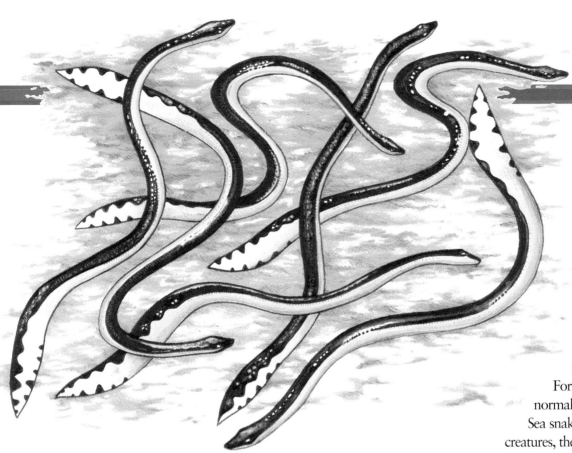

The largest group of sea snakes was spotted in the Malacca Strait in the South Pacific. This concentration of snakes was nearly 60 miles long.

Sea snakes are air-breathing animals and have developed a specialized lung, one that is considerably larger than the two lungs of their land-locked relatives. If necessary, this single lung allows sea snakes to stay underwater for up to 3 1/2 hours and dive to depths of 100 feet or more. This feature is important in helping sea snakes locate their primary food—eels and small fish.

Although few land snakes are deadly, all sea snakes are venomous (have poison). They use their piercing fangs to inject poison directly into their victims, killing them in just a few moments.

Fortunately, they do not normally attack humans.

Sea snakes are communal creatures, they typically travel in large groups. Large schools of sea snakes are often found far out to sea, writhing and wiggling on the surface of the ocean in great numbers.

There are about fifty varieties of sea snakes—ranging in length from 3 to 8 feet—throughout the world. While most spend their entire lives swimming through the ocean, a few species come on land to lay eggs. Ocean-dwelling sea snakes, however, give birth right in the water.

MARINE IGUANAS

Marine iguanas can be found only on the Galapagos Islands. Mostly black or gray in color with splotches of red, an iguana can grow to 4 feet in length. It is distinguished by a blunt snout, a flat tail used for swimming, and a very clumsy-looking body.

Diving Dragons

When you want to eat, you go to the grocery store, a fast food restaurant, or you open the refrigerator at home. You're able to eat many different kinds of food and are able to find that food in many different places. But, unlike you, the marine iguana eats only one type of food and must swim underwater to find it.

The marine iguana is a remarkable creature simply because it can be found entirely on one group of islands—the Galapagos Islands. This small collection of isolated islands is located 600 miles off the western coast of Ecuador, South America, in the Pacific Ocean. It is home to some of the most unusual plant and animal species in the world. One of those species, the marine iguana, feeds entirely on the algae

that grow on underwater rocks. Because it has partially webbed feet, the marine iguana can easily swim beneath the waves. It also has strong claws that help it hold on to the slippery rocks as it feeds. Occasionally, iguanas will swim out to feed beyond the surf, where their chief enemy, the shark, may catch an unsuspecting diner.

When they dive, iguanas can go as deep as 35 feet below the surface, although most will search for food on rocks 15 to 20 feet deep. Although they can stay underwater a long time, most iguanas will remain submerged (underwater) for about 15 to 20 minutes while feeding. Interestingly, the

Female marine iguanas dig tunnels as deep as two feet under the sand to lay their eggs.

This can be dangerous for the iguana—the tunnels could collapse at any moment.

marine iguana is the only lizard that uses the sea as its only source of food.

When they're not eating, marine iguanas will gather in tight bunches on the rocky shore, often piling on top of one another. Here, they bask in the sun, raising their body temperatures to between 95 and 99 degrees F before diving in the cool ocean waters to search for food.

While they sun themselves, small red crabs frequently crawl over and around the iguanas. These crabs use their pinchers to remove small blood-sucking ticks from the iguana's skin. The ticks are an

important part of the crabs' diet.

Although a marine iguana looks fearsome, it is a mild-mannered creature. Occasionally, however, males will engage in short territorial fights in which they butt their heads together. Sometimes males will push each other around with their heads until one gives up and retreats.

Most of the time, however, they would rather sun themselves on the rocks or look for an underwater snack.

When scared, a marine iguana will blow salt water vapor from special glands in its nose—making it look just like a miniature dragon.

BACKSWIMMERS

Rapid Rowers

When you want to travel somewhere, usually you get on a bicycle or ride in a car. Normally you sit or stand right side up and move in a forward direction. For a moment, however, think how it would feel if you had to travel upside down and backward. There's an amazing animal that does just that—and doesn't mind one bit!

The backswimmer is a small insect—about 1/2 inch in length—that lives in ponds and lakes around the world. Pale brown in color, the backswimmer is

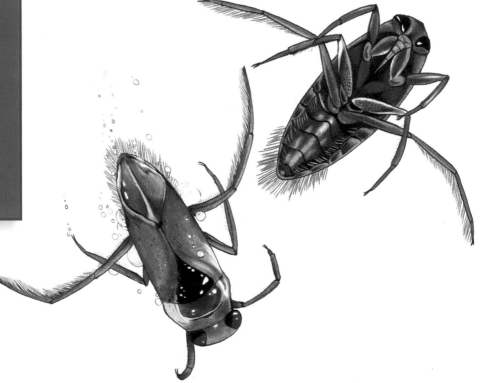

In winter when a pond freezes, backswimmers walk around upside down under the ice.

distinguished by long back legs fringed with fine hairs. These legs look just like a pair of oars on a rowboat.

For much of the day a backswimmer rests upside down just below the surface of the water. It is able to do this by capturing a small bubble of air at the surface and pressing it to its abdomen with a series of small bristles. Since it is also an air-breathing animal it has breathing holes called spiracles along the sides of its abdomen. It presses the captured bubble against those holes and obtains the oxygen it needs. If the backswimmer is frightened or threatened by an enemy, it may dive under the water carrying its bubble with it.

The backswimmer also swims on top of the water. This may be its most distinctive feature. Still upside down, the backswimmer uses its hind legs as oars and quickly propels itself across the surface of the water—away from any enemy.

It also uses this form of locomotion to attack and eat mosquitoes, tadpoles, and small fish. The prey is located by vibrations on the water. Scooting across the water, the backswimmer captures its meal, plunges its beak into the victim, pumps in some digestive juices, and then sucks out the animal's fluids.

Although the backswimmer prefers to swim backward, it also can fly. It flies, however, right side up and forward. A creature that can swim backward and fly forward is an example of the amazing diversity of organisms in the animal kingdom.

KRILL

There are about 85 species of krill, almost all of which inhabit the frigid waters off Antarctica. Krill feed on the billions and billions of tons of plankton that live in the icy waters of this region.

Frozen Food

How many hamburgers or hot dogs can you eat at one time? Two? Four? Ten? Like most people, your limit is probably two or three at a single sitting (you know what happens when you eat too many). Yet, in the Antarctic Ocean, whales will eat millions of a tiny sea creature—all in one gulp! It's not the whales that are distinctive, but the animals they eat—krill.

Krill are small, shrimp-like creatures that live in some of the coldest waters on the planet. A pair of eyes, long antennae, and eight pairs of branched legs

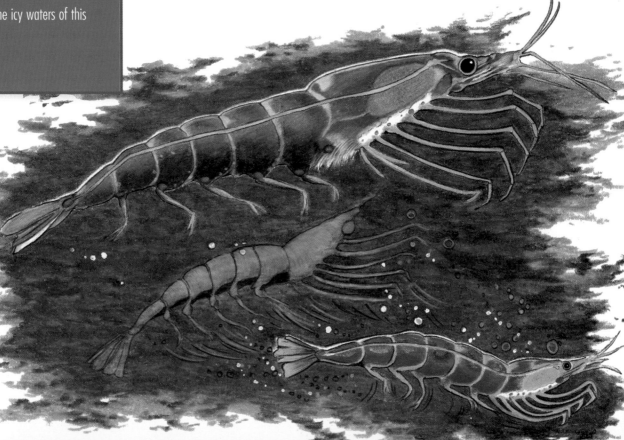

on its 2-inch body make it look like an alien being from a distant world.

What is so amazing about krill is their enormous numbers. Shoals (large groups) of krill commonly swim together through the icy waters of Antarctica. These groups may be as small as a few feet across to more than an acre—a whirling mass of billions and billions of organisms. These shoals may extend for hundreds of yards in circular, oval, or oblong shapes.

Although krill are the main food source of Antarctic whales, they are also a favorite of seals, penguins, sea birds, and other fish.

In fact, many scientists believe that krill are the most important link in the Antarctic food chain— their sheer numbers make them the most valuable food source for a wide variety of animals. Without that food source, there would not be sufficient nourishment for large numbers of polar animals.

Krill are luminescent—their bodies are composed of several light-producing organs. At night they light up and become an enor- mous mass of blue-green. During the day, however, they maintain their reddish color, looking like a gigantic pulsing plant beneath the surface.

Krill are an important food source for the animal populations of the Antarctic and are being con- sidered as a potential food for humans, too. Because krill are high in protein, low in fat, and are readily abundant, several nations are developing plans to harvest these little creatures.

This could be dangerous in that some species of whales subsist almost entirely on krill and therefore may lose an important food source. To feed humans, we may be removing an essential and necessary food from the "table" of other animals, putting them at risk of elimination.

There are about 30 species of lampreys found in the temperate regions of the northern and southern hemispheres. Some live in salt water, others in fresh water. All lampreys, however, begin their lives in fresh water. As they grow, some move down rivers and into the ocean.

Harmful Hitchhikers

When people travel they may drive, ride, or fly. After they arrive at their destination they usually don't destroy their car, bicycle, or airplane. However, there is an animal that does just that—one that "catches" a ride with another animal, and slowly kills its host as they travel together. This hitchhiker, the lamprey, is a most unfriendly swimmer.

One look at a lamprey and you're likely to say that it's one of the ugliest creatures you've ever seen. A lamprey looks like an eel with a slimy scaleless body that can grow to between 6 and 40 inches long.

Its body has no bones whatsoever. In fact, a lamprey's

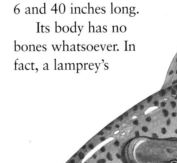

entire body is made of cartilage—the same rubbery material that shapes your nose. Most importantly, a lamprey does not have a jaw. Its head ends in a large funnel-like mouth. It is this mouth that makes the lamprey a very dangerous animal.

The lamprey's circular mouth is filled with dozens of pointed teeth. There are even teeth scattered across its muscular tongue. To feed, the lamprey searches for fish in lakes or rivers. When it locates one, it attaches itself to the side of the fish with its suction-like mouth. It then begins to scrape the fish's skin with its tongue and teeth. The fish begins to bleed, and the lamprey sucks up the blood.

The lamprey may remain attached for weeks or even months, traveling on its host wherever it goes and enjoying a free meal at the same time.

Eventually, the lamprey obtains all the food it needs and detaches itself from its host. At other times, lampreys may continue traveling and feeding until the host is killed.

In some parts of the world—the Great Lakes region of the United States, for example—lampreys have become a serious ecological problem. They multiply rapidly, attach themselves to large numbers of fish, and kill off entire populations of aquatic life. In recent years, a special poison has been developed to control this traveling pest.

Lampreys spend much of their lives swimming as an "attachment" to a fish. While they are capable of swimming on their own, they prefer to hitch a ride on an unsuspecting host. Unfortunately, this turns out to be a "death trip" for the helpful fish.

Fantastic Fact

The ancestors of lampreys have been traced back for 400 to 450 million years.

The sucker mouth of the lamprey is so strong it can pull itself up over rocks or vertical walls.

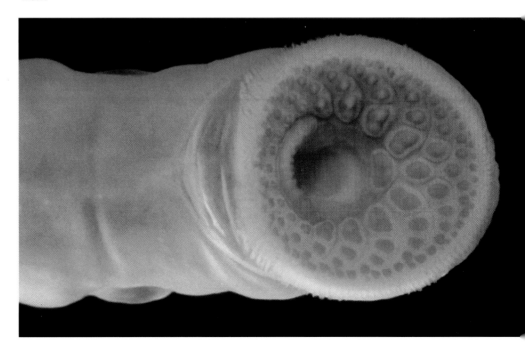

SCALLOPS

There are approximately 300 species of scallops living around the world. Since they prefer shallow water, their shells are often washed up on shore, particularly after severe ocean storms.

Speeding Shells

Lots of people enjoy eating seafood. Many people order lobster, crab, and other kinds of fish when they go out to eat. One of the most popular seafoods is the scallop, a shellfish common along the Atlantic Coast. Interestingly enough, scallops are rapid swimmers. Those you find on your plate in a restaurant, however, weren't fast enough!

Scallops are part of a group of animals called **bivalves**—animals with two shells. Varying in size from 1 to 8 inches, the 300 species of scallops can be

found throughout the world, typically living in shallow waters. Their shells, covered with ridges and corrugations, are pink, red, or yellow. The wavy edges of the shell are where we get the term "scalloped," which also describes a specific way some fabrics are cut.

Scallops lie on the sea bed with their shells open. Frequently, however, they zip through the water just like small jet-propelled submarines. To do this, a scallop opens its shell and fills the interior space with water. The powerful muscle inside quickly contracts, pulling the valves shut and shooting water out from behind. The scallop speeds forward through the water.

Fantastic Fact

A scallop can lose all of its eyes and re-grow them in two months.

Depending on which way a scallop wants to go, it can dart forward or backward. Its motion, however, is erratic and side to side—resembling a saucer sinking in a container of water. Nevertheless, its jets of water are so strong it can blow away an approaching (and hungry) crab.

One of the most distinguishing features of this animal is its rows of tiny eyes along the edge of its mantle (fleshy skin that lines the inside of the shell). Depending on the species, scallops have between 30 and 100 well-developed eyes.

Most bivalves have two muscles, but the scallop has only one. It is this single muscle that is consumed by people around the world. Although the scallop is a quick swimmer and is able to dart away from its primary enemies—the starfish and octopus—it may not be quick enough to escape the chef at your favorite seafood restaurant.

GUILLEMOTS

Guillemots are birds of the north. Principally located in and around the North Sea, they can be found as far south as Portugal and North Korea. In many ways they resemble a duck, growing to 16 inches in length and sporting dark brown feathers and a white belly. Their numbers have decreased in recent years due to polluted oceans and an increasing number of oil spills.

Bathing Birds

Most birds live on land or up in trees. There they make their nests, raise their young, and search for food to feed themselves. When we think of birds, we think of creatures with wings that can fly through the air, traveling from place to place. Soaring, swooping, and diving, these magnificent creatures can be found on every continent in the world and in almost every back yard. But have you ever

seen a bird that flies underwater? The guillemot is a penguin-like bird which is able to do just that!

When it's not feeding, the guillemot lives near the water, building its nests on narrow ledges of towering cliffs. The nests of a guillemot colony, often hundreds of birds, are jammed so close together they are almost on top of one another.

Because they live by the sea, guillemots feed on many types of marine creatures including fish, sand eels, shrimp, crabs, mollusks, and worms. Since fish make up a major portion of their diet, they have developed a distinctive way of catching their dinner. Floating on the water, guillemots will kick their feet, partially spread their wings, and dip their heads.

This action pushes the birds underwater, where they use their

Fantastic Fact

Unlike most other birds, guillemots survive in extremely cold weather. The temperature can drop well below zero and most guillemots do not have to migrate to warmer climates.

wings for propulsion (pushing them forward) and their feet for steering. Here, the birds swoop, glide, and "fly" through the water just as they do in the air. The birds are so fast that fish are usually captured in the birds' beaks after short underwater chases.

Guillemots can travel almost as fast underwater as they can in the air. You can imagine how surprised fish might be when they see a whole flock of these birds swooping after them underwater.

Although guillemots spend a lot of time underwater, they can be found bobbing on top of the waves, too. Here, they rest between dives.

Like many other water birds, guillemots have waterproof feathers that are coated with a special oil to help keep them dry. The feathers are shed once each year and new ones are grown. As the new feathers are growing, guillemots are unable to fly or swim and must feed close to shore to obtain the food they need. The feathers grow fast, however, and soon the guillemots are able to soar over the waves and "fly" under the sea.

DEVIL FISH

Beautiful in "flight," these graceful swimmers can be found in tropical and subtropical oceans around the world. Many large aquariums and oceanariums throughout the United States have devil fish on display, too.

Gentle Giants

Have you ever seen an eagle or hawk lazily gliding through the skies on currents of air? It seems to float on the wind, slowly winging its way across the sky. It can glide with the greatest of ease, occasionally flapping its wings or hovering over the trees.

There's an amazing creature that seems to glide through the water, swooping and soaring through the ocean. It's the devil fish—a relative of sharks, rays, and skates.

The devil fish has a flattened body with large triangular fins that look exactly like wings. A large mouth framed by enormous "horns" makes this creature look terrifying

and menacing. Sailors used to think this animal was one of the most dangerous in the ocean, hence its name. It is, however, only dangerous to small fish, crustaceans, and plankton, which it scoops into its mouth as it swims.

Devil fish are also known as mantas—the Spanish word for "blanket"—which refers to their widespread shape and size. Manta rays, the largest of the devil fish, measure up to 22 feet across. The smallest member of this group is the Australian pygmy ray which reaches a width of only 2 feet across.

Devil fish spend most of their time swimming in small groups of two or three, although they sometimes congregate in schools. Typically, they swim near the surface of the water with slow flapping motions of their gigantic pectoral fins. They often resemble enormous birds gracefully "flying" through the sea. Some people think they even look like colossal bats. As a result, they are sometimes referred to as "batfish."

Fantastic Fact

The largest recorded devil fish measured 60 feet across and weighed 5,000 pounds.

One of the most unusual "tricks" of these immense creatures is to leap high into the air, falling back to the ocean with a loud "whap!"—just like the sound you make when you do a "belly flop" off a diving board. The sound of these animals hitting the water can be heard for miles across a calm sea. No one is quite sure why they display this unusual behavior. It just adds to our appreciation and awe of these magnificent "eagles of the ocean."

Purple sea snails live in the tropical waters of the Atlantic, Pacific, and Indian Oceans. Typically, they live in large groups floating together over great distances. Often, after violent ocean storms, quantities of their shells can be found washed up on island beaches.

Slimy Sailors

Have you ever floated on a raft at the beach, swimming pool, or lake? It's quite relaxing to lie on that cushion of air and pass the day away. How would you like to do it for your entire life? In fact, how would you like to float *upside down under a raft* for your whole life? The purple sea snail is one of the few

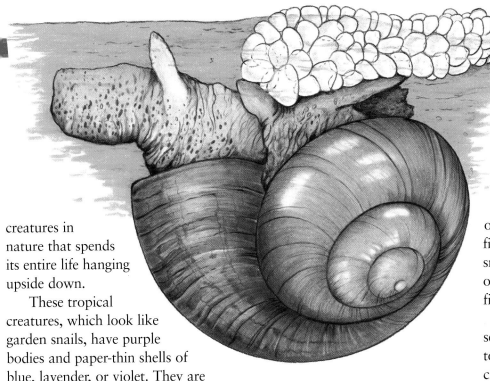

creatures in nature that spends its entire life hanging upside down.

These tropical creatures, which look like garden snails, have purple bodies and paper-thin shells of blue, lavender, or violet. They are seldom more than 2 inches in length and can be found in large numbers in the warm waters of the Atlantic, Pacific, and Indian oceans.

The purple sea snail hangs upside down by creating a small bubble raft. It secretes (oozes) froth from its foot, which traps air into a collection of bubbles. The bubbles are coated with a special mucus (slime) that hardens into a jelly-like substance. The snail glues all the bubbles together into a raft-like structure from which it hangs upside down. The snail spends its life floating along on ocean currents or carried around by ocean winds.

At first glance, you may think this little creature is quite harmless, but don't tell that to a jellyfish! Purple sea snails love to eat jellyfish. While they are floating, the snails can detect the presence of nearby jellyfish through special sense organs located near their mouths. Although sea snails have no eyes, they are quite good at finding their favorite food.

After a jellyfish is located, the sea snail releases a purple dye that anesthetizes (stuns) the jellyfish. Temporarily immobilized, the jellyfish's tentacles (with their stinging cells) are eaten by the snail until only the gas-filled float of the jellyfish remains. After feeding, the sea snail lays as many as 3 million eggs on the underside of the dead jellyfish.

Sometimes it is difficult for the sea snail to locate enough jellyfish to eat. During those times, these creatures become cannibalistic— eating members of their own colony in order to survive.

All purple sea snails are born as males. As they grow, they all become females.

PUFFER FISH

Puffer fish can be found in many of the tropical seas of the world, typically living in and among coral reefs. Here, they eat barnacles, sea snails, crabs, and worms. If taken out of the water, they fill their bellies with air instead of water.

Balloon Bodies

Stand in front of a full-length mirror and look at yourself. Now, inflate your lungs with as much air as you can and observe yourself once more. You'll probably notice little difference between your "deflated" body and your "inflated" body. But how do you think you would look if you could take in enough air to blow yourself up to twice your normal size?

Puffer fish, sometimes known as balloon fish, globe fish, blow fish, or swell fish, inflate their bodies to twice their normal size by taking in large quantities of water. They do this as a form of protection. Puffer fish have a very small gill capacity. They swim slowly and use little energy while swimming.

When threatened, these fish fill up their bellies with water (an 8-inch fish may take in as much as one quart of water), holding the water until the danger passes. By enlarging themselves with water and doubling their size, they appear to be much larger (and meaner) than they really are—thus fooling any would-be predators.

Although most predators would leave a larger prey alone, these clever creatures have another added defense—poison. Puffers are some of the most poisonous of all marine animals. They carry tetraodon-toxin, a powerful nerve poison that causes a violent and rapid death when ingested. This poison is carried in the puffer's liver, reproductive organs, and intestines.

One of the most widely known of all puffer fish is the porcupine fish. When this fish—normally 1 to 2 feet in length—blows itself up, dozens of sharp spines stand out from its body. Each spine is about 2 inches long. These spines serve as protection from the fish's enemies.

Occasionally, however, an unsuspecting (or very hungry) shark will eat one of these fish. The porcupine fish may then inflate itself inside the shark's mouth where it remains stuck for some time—severely injuring the shark. If the shark survives this encounter, it will have learned a very valuable lesson.

Fantastic Fact

In Japan, puffer fish (known as *fugu*) are eaten as a delicacy. Specially trained cooks remove the poisonous parts before the fish are served. Still, every year, dozens of people die from eating this fish.

Sea otters were once almost hunted to near extinction for their fur. Once ranging along the entire Pacific Coast from Mexico up and around to Japan, their numbers are significantly lower today. Although laws are in place to protect them, those laws must be enforced to ensure the survival of this valuable species.

Furry Floaters

Have your parents ever told you not to play with your food? Well, you're about to meet an animal that not only plays with its food, but does so while it's swimming on its back.

The sea otter is a marine mammal that seldom comes on shore. It spends most of its time in small herds off the rocky shores of California, Alaska, and several northern Japanese islands. Long ago, there were many more sea otters than there are today. That's because the fur of the sea otter was highly prized. Fur hunters killed off millions of these animals before tough laws were passed in 1910 and 1911 to protect this valuable creature from extinction.

The fur of a sea otter is dense, thick, and glossy. It ranges in color from dark brown to black. A sea otter's head, throat, and chest are white.

Most interesting is how a sea otter's fur keeps it warm. Sea otters differ from other marine animals in that they have no fat or blubber under their skin to protect them. Air is trapped in their fur, acting as a protective barrier or insulation from the cold water. If the fur becomes covered with oil or other pollutants, it loses its insulating properties and the sea otter dies from exposure (it has no protection from cold water).

A sea otter spends most of its day floating on its back in offshore kelp beds. While it's resting or sleeping, it wraps strands of kelp around itself so it doesn't drift away. Every so often it will dive beneath the water—often to depths of 100 feet—to capture crabs, mussels, clams, abalones, and sea urchins for food. It will also grab a small rock or flat stone in its short paws.

When it returns to the surface, the sea otter floats on its back, uses its chest as a table, and uses the stone to crack open shellfish it has gathered from the ocean floor. In fact, the only time the sea otter doesn't float on its back is when swimming away from danger or diving for food.

Fantastic Fact

To survive, most sea otters need to eat about 20 pounds of food a day (that's one-fourth of their total body weight).

PROTECTING SURPRISING SWIMMERS

There are several organizations working to help preserve animal habitats around the world, including aquatic habitats. The following groups are good sources of information. Contact them and ask for material on how you can become involved in their efforts.

NOAA Marine Debris Information Office

The Center for Marine Conservation
1725 De Sales Street NW
Washington, DC 20036
Provides a variety of brochures, posters, and slides about the dangers, and necessary clean-up, of marine pollution. Produces several classroom games, lesson plans, and other free materials.

Throughout the pages of this book you have met some spectacular animals. You've been introduced to an animal that plays with its food while floating on its back, one that drifts across the ocean on a "home-made" raft, another that is jet-propelled, and even one that can swim upside down and backward. The ways in which these creatures swim are part of how they have learned to survive in their special habitat—the water.

An animal's **habitat** is the place where it lives. That place may be a small pond in the mountains, a large expanse of open ocean in the South Pacific, or a rocky shoreline off the California coast. An animal's habitat supplies everything that animal needs for its survival. Those needs may include food, water, light, proper temperature, and some form of protection or shelter from the elements. Oceans, lakes, rivers, and streams are just a few of the special habitats in which animals live.

If an animal's habitat is harmed, destroyed, or polluted, it may mean danger for that animal. It may not be able to locate the food it needs to survive. It may not be able to protect itself from its enemies. It may not be able to mate and reproduce another generation of its kind. The destruction of some habitats is a natural occurrence in nature. In too many cases, however, habitats are threatened or eliminated because of human activity. When oil tankers run aground, the seeping oil threatens hundreds of marine organisms. When ponds and marshes are drained for housing projects, wetland creatures are threatened. When garbage and waste products are dumped into the ocean, fish life may be eliminated.

When an animal's habitat is destroyed, an animal species may be lost forever, never to return. Protecting the habitats of all animals—including surprising swimmers—not only makes sense, but also helps ensure their survival for generations. What we do today has an impact on how well many animals will survive in the future.

Marine Iguanas

International Wildlife Coalition

Whale Adoption Project
634 North Falmouth Highway
Box 388
North Falmouth, MA 02566
Works to preserve the dwindling populations of various whale species. Provides information on how you and your classmates can "adopt" a whale.

National Wildlife Federation

1400 16th Street NW
Washington, DC 20036
Works to preserve and properly manage wildlife resources around the world. A strong advocate of numerous conservation issues.

Preserving animal habitats is a challenge for all humans, but it's a challenge we can meet by working together. I invite you to work with your parents, your teacher, your classmates, and other people in your community. Wherever you live, you can make a difference. Here are some things you may want to consider:

First, look for and learn about the habitats of various aquatic animals in your part of the country. You may wish to read other books like this one or talk with your teacher or parents about the fish, insects, or amphibians that live near you. If possible, you may want to visit one or more of these habitats. Observe, but do not disturb, these animals.

People working together do make a difference! Your interest and enthusiasm can help alert others to important conservation issues. The "surprising swimmers" of the world are counting on you.

You have met 12 animals that have distinctive ways of swimming. They may swim upside down, they may swim by "flying," or they may swim by hitching a ride with another animal. However these creatures travel, they are examples of the wide diversity (or variety) of animals with which we live. Here is a list of other animals (and one plant) that are also surprising swimmers. You may see some of these in a nearby zoo or aquarium. You can learn more about them by visiting your school library or the public library in your town or city.

BEAVER
When a beaver swims underwater, a special transparent eyelid slides over its eyes to protect them. These eyelids act just like a pair of goggles.

HIPPOPOTAMUS
This 4-ton animal can swim and remain submerged underwater for up to 30 minutes.

COCONUT
Coconuts are the largest of all seeds. When they drop into the water, they may float thousands of miles across the ocean before landing on a distant shore and sprouting.

DIVING BEETLE
This ferocious hunter can swim underwater with another animal twice its size locked in its powerful jaws.

WEDDELL SEAL
This seal is a supreme diver. It's able to dive under the polar ice cap to depths of nearly 2,000 feet.

DIVING BELL SPIDER
This spider collects a large bubble of air at the surface of a pond, takes it underwater, and lives, eats, and sleeps in this special chamber.

SALMON
When it's time to mate and lay eggs, this fish will swim 2,000 miles up a river to return to the exact pool or stream where it was born.

CORMORANT
This sea bird can "fly" underwater for more than one minute, reaching depths of 100 feet.

OCTOPUS
One kind of octopus can make itself completely transparent while swimming.